GOD'S *Great* PLAN

Written by Melissa Cutrera   *Illustrated by* Matthew Sample II

Shepherd Press

God's Great Plan
© 2013 by Melissa Cutrera

Illustrated by Matthew Sample II

Hard Cover ISBN: 9781936908813
eBook ISBN
Mobi format: ISBN 9781936908837
ePub format: ISBN 9781936908820

Published by Shepherd Press
P.O. Box 24
Wapwallopen, Pennsylvania 18660

Unless otherwise indicated, all Scripture are taken from The Holy Bible, English Standard Version. Copyright ©2001 by Crossway Bibles, a division of Good News Publishers. Used by permission. All rights reserved. Italics or bold text within Scripture quotations indicate emphasis added by author.

Cover design by Tobias' Outerwear for Books

First Printing, 2013

Printed in the United States of America

JO 22 21 20 19 18 17 16 15 14 13 12 11
14 13 12 11 10 9 8 7 6 5 4 3 2 1

NIVRIDRAHCIR

Library of Congress Cataloging-in-Publication Data

Cutrera, Melissa.

God's great plan / by Melissa Cutrera ; illustrated by Matthew Sample II.

pages cm

ISBN 978-1-936908-81-3 (print book
ISBN 978-1-936908-83-7 (kindle

format) -- ISBN 978-1-936908-82-0 (epub format) 1.

Salvation--Christianity--Juvenile literature. 2. Bible stories, English.

I. Title.
BT751.3.C88 2013
234--dc23
2013028663

eBook information: Go to: http://www.shepherdpress.com/ebooks

GOD'S *Great* PLAN

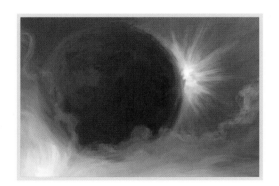

God made the light, the water, the sky.

He called out the land, the trees that grow high.

God hung the sun, the moon, and the stars;

Galaxies, comets, Jupiter, Mars.

Next, God made birds and fish in the seas;
Lizards and llamas and cute chimpanzees.

Lastly, God picked up some dirt from the land,

And with it He formed in His image a man.

He made for the man a helper and wife
And gave them a garden with His tree of life.

The man's name was Adam, and Eve was his bride.
God was their friend, and they walked by His side.

God gave the man just this one rule to follow:

He said there was one fruit that they shouldn't swallow.

Along came a serpent to tempt and deceive;

He lied about God when he whispered to Eve.

He told her to taste the fruit shiny and bright.

She did, and she turned to give Adam a bite.

From that moment on things were never the same;
The whole world was filled up with sadness and shame.

Everything scary came from that dark day,
When people decided to go their own way.

So now you and I and everyone else
Break God's commands and serve only ourselves.

We deserve to be punished for all of our sin,
Because we ignore Him again and again.

God knew this would happen before time began;
To rescue His people was always His plan.

Because of His love, He sent Jesus, His Son,

Who took on Himself all the wrong that we've done.

Although He was God, He became just like us;

He got hungry and tired, but He didn't fuss.

He always obeyed, and He did what was right;

He loved God the Father with heart, soul, and might.

Yes, Jesus was perfect right up to the end,
When He was arrested, betrayed by a friend.

Nailed to a cross, where He suffered and died,

He was mocked as He hung like the thieves by His side.

Punished by God for the bad things we do,

He died in our place so that we could be new.

Jesus is God, so Death couldn't win.

Instead He beat death and overcame sin.

So after three days, He rose from the dead.

He walked and He talked and He even ate bread.

He promised to send us a Helper to guide

Then went up to heaven to sit at God's side.

Now each one who trusts in Christ Jesus alone
Is forgiven of sin and made one of God's own.

The Helper, the Spirit, is changing our hearts
To make us like Jesus, who set us apart.

His life makes us righteous; His death sets us free;

His rising and reign give us hope perfectly.

He's praying for us and preparing a place
Where we'll live forever with the God of all grace.